Endpapers:
Waves at Matsushima,
Screen painting by Sotatsu, detail,
Freer Gallery of Art

THE
ART OF
japan

SHIRLEY GLUBOK

Designed by Gerard Nook
Special Photography by Alfred Tamarin

THE MACMILLAN COMPANY • COLLIER-MACMILLAN LIMITED, LONDON

The Author gratefully acknowledges the assistance of:
JOHN A. POPE, Director, Freer Gallery of Art
MONEY HICKMAN, Fellow for Research, and EMILY BIEDERMAN, Assistant,
Department of Asiatic Art, Museum of Fine Arts, Boston
SHIGETAKA KANEKO, Tokyo National Museum
JAPAN CULTURAL SOCIETY, Tokyo
JAPAN SOCIETY, New York
ALAN SMULEN and MARK OSHIMA
And especially the helpful cooperation of:
HAROLD P. STERN, Assistant Director, Freer Gallery of Art

Other books by Shirley Glubok:
THE ART OF ANCIENT EGYPT
THE ART OF LANDS IN THE BIBLE
THE ART OF ANCIENT GREECE
THE ART OF THE NORTH AMERICAN INDIAN
THE ART OF THE ESKIMO
THE ART OF ANCIENT ROME
THE ART OF AFRICA
ART AND ARCHAEOLOGY
THE ART OF ANCIENT PERU
THE ART OF THE ETRUSCANS
THE ART OF ANCIENT MEXICO
KNIGHTS IN ARMOR
THE ART OF INDIA
THE FALL OF THE AZTECS
THE FALL OF THE INCAS
DISCOVERING TUT-ANKH-AMEN'S TOMB
DISCOVERING THE ROYAL TOMBS AT UR
HOME AND CHILD LIFE IN COLONIAL DAYS

Cover illustrations: paintings on silk, Freer Gallery of Art.
Front: A Woman Walking in a Breeze, by Toyoharu, detail.
Back: Mt. Fuji—Fisherboy in a Willow Tree, by Hokusai. Photographs by Alfred Tamarin.

The Macmillan Company
866 Third Avenue, New York, New York 10022
Collier-Macmillan Canada, Ltd., Toronto, Ontario
Library of Congress catalog card number: 75-89584
FIRST PRINTING

J apan is a string of islands in the Pacific Ocean off the coast of Asia. There are four main islands and hundreds of smaller ones. In the interior of the larger islands are steep mountains and rounded hills. The millions of people in Japan live in the valleys and in the narrow plains along the seacoast. The beautiful mountains and rich valleys with rivers, streams and waterfalls are reflected in Japanese art.

Japan has one of the oldest traditions in the world. The Japanese emperor comes from a line of sovereigns which goes back about two thousand years.

Over the centuries the country's capital has been moved from the city of Nara to Kyoto, and finally to Edo, now called Tokyo.

Heavenly Beings on Clouds, wood, Byodyo-in, Kyoto

The earliest culture we know in Japan is called *Jomon*. It is named for the twisted rope decorations on clay pots made by a people who lived about four thousand years ago. The Jomon people also made small figurines. This one has a heart-shaped head, a large triangular nose and a tiny mouth.

Detail of figure,
Yamazaki Collection

About seventeen hundred years ago Japanese emperors and other important officials were buried in stone chambers covered with great mounds of earth.
Hollow clay cylinders called *haniwa* were set around the foot of the mounds to
strengthen the sides and keep the earth from washing away.

Many haniwa were modeled after human and animal forms. To make this
horse, the artist joined four cylinders representing the legs to a fifth cylinder
forming the body. Round openings were made for the eyes and nostrils. The
horse is equipped with saddle, bridle and stirrups.

Above is a haniwa model of an early Japanese house.

The first haniwa were simple cylinders. Later, figures were modeled on top. It is thought that in earlier times servants were buried with their dead masters. The haniwa figures may symbolize these attendants.

The cylinders were hollow so that they would bake evenly when put in the kiln, a very hot oven. Openings for the eyes and mouth allowed the hot gases to escape during baking and prevented the cylinders from cracking.

The lively figures at left seem to be dancing and singing, yet they are very simply formed. The haniwa soldier is protected by ancient armor and a tall helmet. He holds his sword ready for battle. The figure at right has a jolly expression. His lips turn up in a smile.

Haniwa were made at a time before the Japanese had writing. They provide valuable information about early Japanese people.

Avery Brundage Collection,
M. H. de Young Memorial
Museum, San Francisco,
photograph by Alfred Tamarin

Kofuku-ji, Nara,
photograph, Japan Cultural
Society, Tokyo

The Buddhist religion began in India and spread through China into Japan. Early Buddhist art in Japan is very Chinese in feeling.

This large seated statue represents Kannon, a Buddhist god who gathered the faithful and led them to Paradise. He is noted for his mercy. The statue is wood, covered with gold. Kannon is seated on a lotus throne. The lotus flower is symbolic of Buddha.

Kannon sits deep in thought, a flaming crown on his head. He has six extra hands, a sign of superhuman power. Two hands are pressed together in prayer. In Buddhist statues each position of the hands has a different meaning. The small jewel between Kannon's eyes represents "the third eye of wisdom."

The wooden figure riding a fierce dragon is a messenger of Fudo, one of the five kings who protect the Buddhist world from evil.

Mt. Koya, Wakayama Prefecture
photograph, Japan Cultural Society, Tokyo

This bronze standing figure is the Bodhisattva Moonlight. Bodhisattvas are beings of complete enlightenment who dedicated themselves to relieving the misery of the world. The figure looks like a Chinese statue. It is larger than life-size and is one of the finest bronze statues in the world.

One of the Bodhisattva's hips is thrust outward, giving a slight sway to the body. The raised hand is in the position of holding a lotus flower. The drapery covering the figure's arms and legs seems thin and transparent. Rich jewels and a crown adorn the statue.

The Bodhisattva stands in a temple in Nara. In front of the statue are offerings brought by worshipers. The flowers in the vase have been arranged in a special way. The art of flower arrangement, still practiced everywhere in Japan, started in Buddhist temples.

Yakushi-ji,
photograph by Alfred Tamarin

At right is a wooden statue representing the Buddha Whose Light Shines Everywhere. The statue wears a high crown and is covered with gold. Most Japanese statues are of wood because stone is scarce in Japan.

The face of this Buddha is beautifully shaped. The long earlobes symbolize Buddha's royal birth.

Buddha grew up in a palace in northern India. He was protected from misery and pain, until one day he wandered forth from his palace and came upon a suffering man, a sick man and a dead man. He decided to give up his life of luxury and devote himself to helping other people. After many years of praying, fasting and teaching, he reached enlightenment and founded the Buddhist religion. The name Buddha means the enlightened one, he who knows all things.

By Unkei, Enjo-ji, Nara, photograph, Japan Cultural Society, Tokyo

The largest wooden structure ever built is this Buddhist temple in Nara. The original temple, erected seven hundred years ago, was even bigger, but it burned down and had to be replaced. In the building is a statue of the Buddha, the largest bronze statue in the world.

The temple has a tiled roof. A large stone lantern stands in front of the entrance. To the right is an open pavilion with a basin where worshipers rinse

Daibutsuden, Todai-ji,
photograph by Alfred Tamarin

their hands and mouths before entering. Early Japanese buildings were constructed by excellent craftsmen who fitted the beams together without using nails.

In a Buddhist temple in Kyoto stands a superb wooden statue which is Japan's National Treasure Number One. It represents the Miroku Bosatsu, the Buddha of the Future, who will someday come to save the world.

The position of the right hand with the fingers gracefully raised to the chin shows that the figure is in deep thought. Soft folds of cloth fall over the legs and the throne in a waterfall design. The Miroku's foot rests on a lotus petal.

The earliest wooden statues were carved from a single tree trunk. This one was made from several blocks of wood, carved separately and joined together.

Koryu-ji,
photograph by Alfred Tamarin

This wooden warrior represents one of the four guardian kings who watch over the four directions of the Buddhist universe. He is poised with his sword ready to strike down those who might do evil to the temple or to Buddhism. He wears Chinese armor, of a type never actually worn by the Japanese. His hair is in a topknot of the Chinese style and a demon mask is attached to his belt. The warrior stands in a temple in Nara.

The three figures at right, in vigorous poses, are part of a set of twelve guardian generals. Their eyes are of colored glass, giving them a lifelike look. Guardian figures were made to look fierce. Their purpose was to protect Buddha and frighten off evil. If a person was true to his faith then the figure would be his protector.

Kofuku-ji,
photograph, Japan Cultural
Society, Tokyo

Junishinsho, Kakuon-ji, Kamakura

15

Descent of Amida, detail,
Mt. Koya, Wakayama Prefecture,
photograph, Japan Cultural Society, Tokyo

It is believed that a Buddha lives in a glorious paradise where jewels and flowers hang from every tree. The Buddha, called Amida, descends from the heavens to greet the faithful as they enter his paradise. His attendants, Bodhisattvas, accompany him.

At left is a detail, or part, of a painting on silk, showing Bodhisattvas floating to earth on swirling clouds. One carries the sacred lotus flowers. Another figure has his hands pressed together in prayer. Their heads are encircled by halos, or rings of light.

One of the leading supporters of Buddhism in Japan in its early stages was young

Prince Shotoku. He became known as Crown Prince "Sage Virtue."

This portrait, or likeness, depicts Shotoku as the Bodhisattva Jizo, the protector of children. Jizo always carries a rod with six jingling rings. The sound warned all animals and insects of his approach so they could scurry to safety. Jizo did not want to tread accidentally on any living creature.

Shotoku had a great Buddhist temple built in Nara. He studied art so that he could supervise the building of the temple.

He brought Buddhist scholars, priests, artists and craftsmen to Japan from Korea.

Empress Jingo,
Yakushi-ji, Nara

18

Kencho-ji, Kamakura

At left is a wooden statue of an empress who is a goddess of the Shinto religion. Shintoism, the earliest religion in Japan, is based on nature worship, and is practiced only in Japan. Divine spirits are believed to live in the wind, rain, mountains, forest, fields and waterfalls.

For most of its history Japan had both an emperor and a military governor called a *shogun*. In its earliest days the shogun's government was located at Kamakura.

Important lords and generals were often represented in very realistic wooden portrait statues. Above, Hojo Tokiyori, regent of Japan and a leading adviser of a shogun, is shown in court costume with balloonlike trousers, wide sleeves and a tall hat. The statue, composed of several blocks of wood, was constructed in the shape of a pyramid, wide at the bottom and rising to a point at the top.

At a later time military leaders built fortified castles. This one, known as the White Heron, is both elegant and strong. A moat, a deep ditch filled with water, surrounds it. Its massive granite walls are more than fifty feet high. The main tower rises about one hundred feet above the walls. It served as a watchtower with a commanding view of the countryside. There are also three smaller towers; all are connected by an inside corridor. The castle is designed with pointed tile roofs, one over the other.

Himeiji Castle, Hyogo Prefecture,
photograph by Alfred Tamarin

Inside Japanese castles, palaces and homes, rooms are bare and uncluttered. The floors are covered with straw mats called *tatami*. Each mat is about six feet long and three feet wide. The size of a room is described according to the number of tatami that will fit. The walls are of paper, and sliding screens, wooden frames covered with thick paper, separate the rooms. Sliding doors lead to the garden.

The gardens are planned as part of the room decoration, as if they were paintings, and are meant to be enjoyed from indoors. Below is a view of the

Shugakuin Detached Palace, Kyoto,
photograph by Alfred Tamarin

interior of an emperor's palace in Kyoto.

Japanese gardens are considered a form of art and are designed in imitation of mountains, ravines, waterfalls, clouds and oceans. Some gardens are made only of moss. Some are entirely of sand, gravel and rocks.

At the right is a famous Zen rock garden in Kyoto. Zen is a sect of Buddhism that emphasizes simple living and worships no images.

Rocks of different sizes and shapes are carefully arranged on finely raked white gravel. Alongside the garden is a porch where people sit and contemplate, thinking quietly. Some people imagine the rocks as islands in an ocean. To others they might be mountain peaks above the clouds.

Ryoan-ji, Kyoto,
photograph by Alfred Tamarin

Mountains, mists, valleys and rivers are favorite subjects of Japanese painters. This broad landscape is a view of Uji, a village near Kyoto. The early morning sun is coming over the mountains. The painting is not meant to be realistic; it has a dreamlike quality. To the left is the well-known bridge of Uji. A boat floats past the Byodo-in, a temple which is built in the form of a flying phoenix. A tall mountain range rises in the distance. There is only slight color in this painting, primarily made with black ink on paper.

The artist has created a variety of shapes and patterns. The leaves of different trees are indicated by dots and lines. The painting gives a sense of deep valleys and of great distance through the mist.

By Aoki Mokubei,
Tokyo National Museum,
photograph; Japan Cultural
Society, Tokyo

24

The brush used in Japanese painting has a very fine point. A slight difference in pressure varies the thickness of the stroke. The artist works with speed, to give life to the painting.

The angle at which the brush is held makes a great difference. If it is held upright, the line is hard; if held at a slant, the line is softer. The tip of the brush makes a more powerful stroke than the side.

Many Japanese paintings were made on scrolls, long sheets of paper which were kept rolled up. The section of a scroll, below, is

Painting by Sotatsu; calligraphy by Hon-ami Koetsu,
Seattle Art Museum, gift of Mrs. Donald E. Frederick

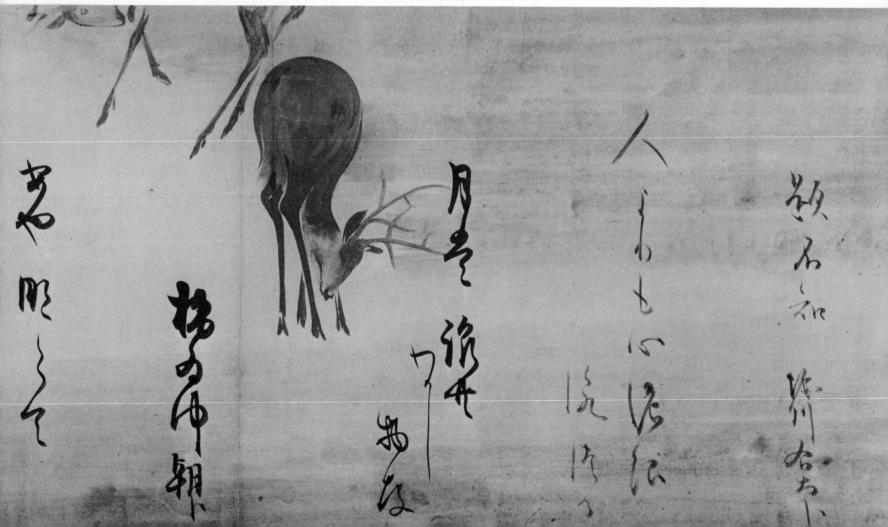

decorated with a herd of deer. The deer are very freely drawn and seem graceful and fast moving.

Calligraphy, or writing, is an important form of art in Japan. The same kinds of brush and ink are used for both painting and calligraphy and every brush stroke is very important. Each character, or sign, has a specific meaning.

Japanese calligraphy came originally from China and was modified in its new land. The Japanese developed additional forms of writing which they combined with the Chinese characters to create their own written language.

The painting at right is in black ink on paper. A baby gibbon hangs from its mother's foot as she swings in a tree.

Attributed to Shugetsu,
Royal Ontario Museum

Japanese poetry was sometimes written on illustrated scrolls. Below is a portrait of a poet. Poets were highly respected at the emperor's court. This one wears stiff court costume. The picture is painted on paper in black ink and colors.

The painting at right illustrates how ink is prepared. The ink is made from lampblack, or from a black substance that comes from burning pine needles. When compressed it forms a black ink stick. Water is dropped onto a stone and the ink stick is rubbed on the stone to make ink. Further drops of water can be added to control the thickness of the ink.

Portrait of Minamoto no Kintada, attributed
to Fujiwara Nobuzane, Freer Gallery of Art

The girl preparing ink sits in typical Japanese fashion, on a quilt. There are no chairs or beds in Japanese homes. Everyone sits on the floor, and people sleep on quilts which are rolled up and kept in a cupboard when not in use. In front of the girl are some scrolls, partly rolled. Behind her is a folding screen with a picture of a river and a tree. These screens are among the few furnishings in a Japanese room.

Outside the house is a plant, and next to it a washbasin with a dipper.

Fifty years after Columbus landed in America three Portuguese travelers reached Japan, the first Europeans ever seen by the Japanese. Portuguese traders and missionaries soon followed.

Japanese artists were fascinated by the big ships and foreign appearance of the Europeans—particularly their height and their long noses.

At left is a screen painting showing the arrival of a Portuguese ship in Japan. The Portuguese were excellent sailors, with the fastest, best-equipped ships in the world. The Japanese were very much interested in these foreign vessels and they painted every detail carefully.

Kobe Municipal Namban Art Museum,
photograph by Alfred Tamarin

The screen above shows the God of Thunder leaping through the air and beating on his drums to create the sound of thunder. His flowing hair and trailing garments suggest a swirling storm. The artist has drawn his body with a feeling of strength and movement. There is a touch of humor in this god, with his sprawling legs and grinning face.

The stories of the lives of princes and priests were often illustrated on scrolls. Below is a scene from the life of Prince Shotoku, showing him as a young boy taking part in an archery contest. The Prince is going to shoot an arrow through five drums lined up in a row. This will prove that he is as strong as the Buddha, who as a young prince had performed a similar feat.

Scrolls also told stories of magic and enchantment. This illustration is from *Tale of a Crane,* a story of a beautiful lady and a lonely man. The lonely man is in his house, sitting in typical Japanese fashion, silently watching a lovely crane leave him. Sometime before, the crane had been captured by a farmer, who was about to kill it. The man saved the bird's life and set it free. A few days later a beautiful lady came to the man's house and stayed with him. Eventually she told him that she was the crane whose life he had saved. Then, turning back into a crane, she flew away.

Sometimes the subjects of the scroll paintings are amusing. This scene is from a famous scroll showing animals taking part in human activities. Animals are bathing in a river. Rabbits scrub a deer's back and a monkey washes another monkey while a rabbit stands by to pour water. These scenes also have a deeper meaning. They were painted by Buddhist priests, and the animals represent religious people who were after too much power. The figures were drawn with simple black lines and quick brushstrokes.

Scroll paintings sometimes show everyday people in everyday scenes. They give us a picture of Japanese life. In this painting a fishmonger, one who sells fish, is arguing with a greengrocer, one who sells fruits and vegetables. Two other men are trying to prevent the angry merchants from fighting. The painting is from a scroll illustrating the customs of Edo, the capital city of Japan (modern Tokyo).

By Hanabusa Itcho,
Honolulu Academy of Arts

An exciting scroll, known as the *Tale of Heiji*, records an important event

in history. About eight hundred years ago two noble families engaged in a bitter

fight for power. The scene shows the courtyard of the imperial palace in Kyoto

Burning of the Sanjo Palace,
Museum of Fine Arts, Boston,
Fenollosa-Weld Collection

which had been set on fire. The mounted attackers are slaughtering the hope-

lessly trapped defenders. The artist has drawn the scene with tremendous sweep

and power, and has paid strict attention to the appearance of each fighter.

Life of Priest Honen, Chion-in, Kyoto, photograph, Japan Cultural Society, Tokyo

Other favorite subjects in scroll paintings were the lives of famous priests and monks. Priest Honen Shonin was a great religious teacher. This section shows some of the priest's attendants and warriors, wearing armor. Japanese armor is made of thin overlapping scales of steel and hard leather. Rows of scales are laced together with colored silk cord, giving a gay appearance to the armor. The inside is lined with padded cloth to make it comfortable to wear. The armor hung loosely over the body, allowing great freedom of movement.

At right is the full suit of armor of a Japanese officer. It is made of more than forty-five hundred scales which are held together by 265 yards of silk braid. Separate metal pieces protect the legs and arms.

The helmet has a bowl with a nose defense and is surmounted by a figure of a dragon between metal antlers. A metal mask guards the warrior's face. Its fierce expression is intended to frighten the enemy.

The Japanese knight in armor was expert at shooting arrows from horseback. In close combat he used a long, slightly curved sword, made of fine steel. Japanese swords have a keen edge and are said to be the finest ever made. Wearing two swords was a sign of high rank. A warrior permitted to wear two swords was called a *samurai*.

The Metropolitan Museum of Art, Rogers Fund, 1904

The custom of tea drinking started in China and was brought to Japan by merchants and scholars who visited China. Tea was considered to cleanse the body, purify the mind and encourage right thinking.

A separate house or a room in the main house is set aside for the tea ceremony. It usually has low doors so that a person must stoop to a humble position to enter.

Every step of the tea ceremony, even the order in which people enter, takes place in a prescribed manner. Special green tea is prepared, mixed, served and drunk according to strict rules. The only conversation permitted is about subjects like art, music and poetry. Simple pots

Freer Gallery of Art

and cups are used to show that beauty can be found in simple objects. The tea bowls are deliberately uneven in shape and often show marks of the potter's hands. This group of objects could have been used in a tea ceremony: an iron kettle, a clay incense container in the shape of a rabbit, a water pot with an arched handle, and a tray for sweets.

In recent years Japanese artists have turned to scenes of the daily activities of ordinary people. At left is a picture of a young man and woman walking in the snow. The man is dressed in a dark kimono, and the young woman wears a kimono with wide sleeves that hang below her knees. Her kimono is held by a wide waistband, called an *obi,* which is arranged in a large fold in back. They wear wooden clogs to protect their feet. At one time, all Japanese wore clogs out of doors. It has always been a custom to leave footwear at the doorstep. One never wears shoes in a Japanese home.

In the scene at right a woman is bathing a child in a washtub. The woman has a typical Japanese hairdo, with ornamental hairpins. The straight lines of her eyebrows add to her

By Harunobu,
The Metropolitan Museum of Art,
Rogers Fund, 1936

beauty. Japanese artists considered a three-quarter view of the face and neckline to be the most beautiful.

These pictures are prints made from blocks of wood. To make a wood-block print the artist first made a drawing with brush and black ink on very thin paper. The drawing was laid face downward on a smooth block of wood. The design on the paper was cut into the wood, coming out in reverse. The background was chipped out, and black printing ink was put on the raised surface of the wood. When a piece of paper was placed on top and rubbed, the design was transferred onto it. Great numbers of prints could be made from the same block, so they could be sold cheaply. The prints were used for books, calendars, billboards and as decorations for homes.

By Utamaro,
Museum of Fine Arts, Boston,
photograph by Alfred Tamarin

This print is an exciting picture of travelers caught in a violent storm. The bamboo trees bend in the wind. Travelers scurry toward the edges of the picture. Rain slants downward in the opposite direction from the swaying trees and the mountainside. The triangular design is repeated in the roofs of the houses. Two men carry a person in a palenquin, an enclosed box supported by poles.

Plays are an important form of entertainment in Japan. In one popular form of theater, called *kabuki,* elaborate stories with music and dancing are enacted on huge stages and performed in brilliant costume. Today only men can be kabuki actors. Women's parts are played by men.

This wood-block print shows a kabuki actor portraying a powerful young man uprooting a bamboo tree. He has great muscles in his arms and legs. Shoots of young bamboo trees can be seen at his feet. There is a sense of great effort as the tree bends under his strength.

The calligraphy in the lower right is the artist's signature. Below it are stamped seals of the artist, the publisher and the collector, or person who owned it.

The Actor Ichikawa Danjuro I
in the Role of Goro,
by Torii Kiyomasu,
Tokyo National Museum

45

The power and movement of a great wave is captured in this famous print. Overhead is a dull-gray sky with faint outlines of clouds. The furious sea threatens two long open boats. The seamen crouch in fear of the crashing waves.

In the distant background is snow-covered Mount Fuji, the highest mountain in Japan. Mount Fuji often appears in Japanese art. It is an almost perfect cone but is not quite as pointed as it looks here. Fuji has always been regarded as a sacred mountain and has become a symbol of Japan. At one time it was an active volcano, but it has not erupted for about three hundred years.

By Hokusai,
The Metropolitan Museum of Art,
The Howard Mansfield Collection,
Rogers Fund, 1936

47

Ama no Hashidate, detail,
by Sesshu,
National Museum, Kyoto

Japanese art reflects the history of the islands and the life of the people. Magnificent religious figures, made hundreds of years ago for temples and shrines, are still worshiped to this day.

The simple interiors of Japanese homes are in harmony with the beauty of nature. Gardens are works of art, whether filled with plants, or rocks and sand. Calligraphy, the tea ceremony and the various schools of flower arrangement, all express the Japanese belief that art should be an inseparable part of life.